Standards-Based Connections
Reading

Grade 1

Carson-Dellosa Publishing, LLC
Greensboro, North Carolina

Credits
Content Editor: Erin McCarthy
Copy Editor: Christine M. Schwab

Visit *carsondellosa.com* for correlations to Common Core, state, national, and Canadian provincial standards.

Carson-Dellosa Publishing, LLC
PO Box 35665
Greensboro, NC 27425 USA
carsondellosa.com

ISBN 978-1-4838-2474-1

01-188151151

Table of Contents

Introduction

Reading comprehension is an essential skill for enabling school, college, and career success. This book focuses on five reading comprehension skills: story elements, summarizing, compare and contrast, cause and effect, and inferring. Emphasized are the reading standards in the Common Core State Standards.

The reading standards set expectations for each grade level and define what students should understand and be able to do. They are designed to be more rigorous and allow for students to justify their thinking. They reflect the knowledge that is necessary for success in college and career readiness. Students who master the standards as they advance through the grades will exhibit the following capabilities:

1. They demonstrate independence.
2. They build strong content knowledge.
3. They respond to the varying demands of audience, task, purpose, and discipline.
4. They comprehend as well as critique.
5. They value evidence.
6. They use technology and digital media strategically and capably.
7. They come to understand other perspectives and cultures.*

How to Use This Book

This book is a collection of grade-appropriate practice pages aligned to the reading sections of the Common Core State Standards for English Language Arts. Included is a skill matrix to show exactly which standards are addressed on the practice pages. Also included are a skill assessment and a skill assessment analysis. Use the assessment at the beginning of the year or at any time you wish to assess your students' mastery of certain standards. The analysis connects each test item to a practice page or set of practice pages so that you can review skills with students who struggle in certain areas.

© Carson-Dellosa • CD-104658

Common Core State Standards Alignment Matrix

Page #	12	13	14	15	16	17	18	19	20	21	22	23	24	25	26	27	28	29	30	31	32	33	34	35	36	37	38	39	40	41	42	43	44	45	46	47	48	49	50	51
1.RL.1				•	•	•						•	•	•	•		•	•			•				•		•												•	•
1.RL.2																				•							•	•		•										
1.RL.3	•	•	•	•	•	•				•			•	•	•	•	•																						•	
1.RL.4																																								
1.RL.5																																								
1.RL.6																																								
1.RL.7	•	•				•	•			•	•																													
1.RL.8																																								
1.RL.9																		•																						
1.RL.10				•				•			•			•		•	•																							
1.RI.1																			•		•			•					•					•			•			
1.RI.2																						•																		
1.RI.3																																		•	•	•	•	•	•	
1.RI.4																						•																		
1.RI.5																													•											
1.RI.6																																								
1.RI.7																								•																
1.RI.8																																								
1.RI.9																																	•		•		•			
1.RI.10																			•				•			•			•		•			•		•		•		

Page #	52	53	54	55	56	57	58	59	60	61	62	63	64	65	66	67	68	69	70	71	72	73	74	75	76	77	78	79	80	81	82	83	84	85	86	87	88	89	90	91
1.RL.1								•			•	•	•	•	•	•		•	•		•		•							•				•	•	•		•		
1.RL.2																						•				•														
1.RL.3											•			•			•				•	•		•	•		•			•		•		•	•					
1.RL.4			•	•						•			•										•	•													•		•	
1.RL.5																																								
1.RL.6																																								
1.RL.7											•		•	•	•			•			•		•	•										•	•	•	•	•	•	
1.RL.8																																								
1.RL.9																																					•			
1.RL.10								•			•						•		•							•	•			•										
1.RI.1	•																							•																
1.RI.2																																								
1.RI.3			•			•		•		•	•																													
1.RI.4																																	•							•
1.RI.5																																								
1.RI.6																																								
1.RI.7																																								
1.RI.8																																								
1.RI.9		•	•			•																																		
1.RI.10					•	•			•																															

© Carson-Dellosa • CD-104658

Molly's Shopping Trip (cont.)

Think about the stores that Molly visited. Describe each setting in a sentence.

Book Store

_____

_____

Grocery Store

_____

_____

Pet Store

_____

_____

Toy Store

_____

_____

☐ I can use illustrations and details in a story to describe its characters, settings, or events.

☐ I can describe characters, settings, and events in a story.

Friends on the Map

When stories are about real places, you can find their settings on a map. Follow the directions.

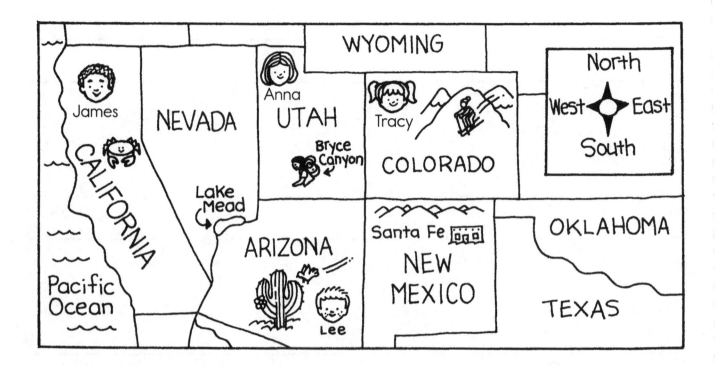

1. Color the state where Anna lives blue.

2. Color the state where Lee lives red.

3. Color the state where James lives green.

4. Color the state where Tracy lives purple.

5. Color the other states yellow.

☐   I can describe characters, settings, and events in a story.

The Dog and the Bone

Look at the story. Circle the answer to each question.

1.   What is the character?

     a dog   a bone

2.   What does the character want?

     to catch a fish   to get a bigger bone

3.   What happens at the end of the story?

     He loses his bone.   He gets scared of water.

☐   **I can ask and answer questions about a text I have read.**
☐   **I can point to the pictures and the text that describe parts of a story.**

Beach Trouble

Penny Packrat is having a bad day at the beach. Help Penny get home. Write the letter for each thing that happens next to its picture in the maze.

a. tripped on a rock
b. sunburned her nose
c. bitten by a crab
d. lost her beach ball
e. at home

Ooof.

❑ I can poin___ ___o the pictures and the text that describe parts of a story.

The Wrong Picture

Look at the books. The titles tell about each character's problem. Draw an **X** on the picture that does not match the book.

1. The Fox and the Grapes

2. The Lost Balloon

3. Too Many Kittens

4. Bad Day at the Beach

Oh, No!

Write the letters on the lines to match each story to its picture.

1. John got a leash. He wanted to take his brand-new puppy for a walk. As John walked into the yard, he cried, "Oh, no!" His sister Jill had taken the puppy out already. _____

a.

2. John pulled on his boots, mittens, and hat. He got his sled and walked to the top of the hill. He looked at the hill. "Oh, no!" he sighed. _____

b.

3. Benji was very hungry. He had played ball with John all morning. He ran to his food bowl. "Oh, no!" panted the puppy. Time to call out for some food! _____

c.

4. Mom wanted to cook eggs for breakfast. She took the carton out and set it on the counter. Benji jumped up. The eggs fell. "Oh, no!" cried Mom. _____

d.

☐   **I can point to pictures and the text that describe parts of a story.**
☐   **I can read prose and poetry.**

A Gift for Mother

Read the story. Answer the questions.

Penny the Packrat was alone in her room. She was feeling sad. She wanted to buy her mother a gift. But, Penny did not have any money in her toy bank. Penny sat down on her bed. What could she do?

Then, Penny smiled and hopped up. She pulled a big bag from under her bed. It held all of her favorite things. Maybe she could use some of them to make a gift.

This is what Penny took out of her bag:

three green buttons   one blue feather

one red ribbon   one brown hat

Penny went to work, and soon she had a surprise for Mother.

1. Who is the main character? _____

2. What is her problem? _____

3. What is the story's setting?_____

4. Color the picture that shows what Penny made to solve her problem.

☐   **I can ask and answer questions about a text I have read.**
☐   **I can describe characters, settings, and events in a story.**

Who Is Lost?

Read the story. Answer the questions.

Shauna looked into her pet's bed. Henry should have been fast asleep. Shauna did not see him. Henry was gone! Where did he go?

Shauna looked all around the room. She looked on the floor. She looked in the closet. She looked under her bed. She could not find Henry.

Shauna felt like crying as she got dressed for school. She reached into an open dresser drawer to pull out a shirt. She touched something soft and furry. Then, she heard a purr. A tongue licked her fingers. Can you guess what was in Shauna's dresser drawer?

1. Who are the characters? _____

2. What is Shauna's problem? _____ _____

3. Where does this story take place? _____

4. What did Shauna find in her dresser drawer?_____

5. Circle Henry:

☐ I can ask and answer questions about a text I have read.
☐ I can describe characters, settings, and events in a story.

The Cat and the Mice

Read the story. Answer the questions on page 26.

Every day, Kitty Cat chased the mice. She liked to tickle them. But, the mice didn't want to be tickled. It made them laugh too much! So, the mice hid inside a hole.

"What can we do?" asked Mother Mouse. "The cat likes to tickle us too much."

"I don't know," said Father Mouse.

"I don't know," said Jimmy Mouse.

"I don't know," said Ramsey Mouse.

"I know," said Maria Mouse. "Let's hang a bell around Kitty's neck. Then, when we hear her coming, we can run."

Everyone cheered. They told Maria Mouse how smart she was.

Then, Ramsey Mouse said, "That is a good idea, but we still have a problem. Who will put the bell on the cat?"

☐   I can read prose and poetry.

The Cat and the Mice (cont.)

Circle the answer to each question.

1. Who are the characters in the story?

    five mice and a cat   five cats   five mice and a dog

2. What is the setting?

    in a school   in a hole   in the forest

3. What is the problem at the beginning of the story?

    The cat laughs at the mice.   The cat tickles the mice too much.

4. What character asks, "What can we do?"

    Maria Mouse   Mother Mouse   Ramsey Mouse

5. What character says, "I know"?

    Maria Mouse   Father Mouse   Jimmy Mouse

6. What is the problem at the end of the story?

    Who will look for food?

    Who will put the bell on the cat?

    Who can tickle the cat?

☐ I can ask and answer questions about a text I have read.
☐ I can describe characters, settings, and events in a story.

The Snowman

Read the story. Circle key words that describe each setting. List them in the chart.

Beth lives in Arizona. It is so hot there, it almost never snows. Her best friend, Tyler, just moved to Michigan. Each winter, it gets cold and snows a lot. When the first snow of the season fell, Tyler was excited. He went outside to build his first snowman.

Tyler wrote to Beth and told her how he built his snowman. First, he rolled a big snowball. Then, he made a smaller one and set it on top. Next, Tyler found two dark pebbles on the ground. He used them to make the eyes. He put his dad's fishing hat on top.

Beth wanted to make a snowman too. But how could she do it without snow? She had an idea. She put on her mother's work gloves. Then, she picked up a big ball of tumbleweed. Tumbleweeds are like dry bushes. Beth put a smaller ball of tumbleweed on top. Next, she found two dark pebbles on the ground. She used them for eyes. Then, she got a red chile pepper and her brother's cowboy hat. Beth used the pepper for a mouth. Then, she put her brother's hat on top.

Beth wrote a letter to Tyler. She told him about her snowman that would never melt!

Beth's Home	Tyler's Home

❏ I can compare and contrast characters in a story.
❏ I can describe characters, settings, and events in a story.
❏ I can read prose and poetry.

Name_____

Watch Out!

Read the story. Circle the correct answer for each question.

Becky Butterfly fluttered over a fence. She landed on a flower. She felt something move nearby. She looked down. A kitten grabbed the flower.

"Uh-oh," Becky thought. So, away she flew! She soared into the sky. She flew out of danger.

1. Who is the story about?

    Brianna Butterfly   Becky Butterfly   Brandy Bug

2. Where did she land?

    on a fence   in a tree   on a flower

3. What tried to catch her?

    a kitten   a boy   a girl

4. Did it catch her?

    yes   no

❑   **I can ask and answer questions about a text I have read.**

28

Name_____

Any Mail Today?

Read the story and look closely at the pictures. Answer the questions. Fill in the blanks to complete the summary.

   Joey watched the mail truck stop at his house. The mail carrier got out and put several things in the mailbox. She waved goodbye and drove away. After she left, this is what Joey found inside the mailbox.

1. Who put mail in the mailbox? _____

2. How many letters were in the mailbox? _____

3. How many packages? _____

4. How many magazines were in the mailbox? _____

_____ found _____ letters, _____

package, and _____ magazines in the mailbox.

□   I can ask and answer questions about a text I have read.

Piñatas

Read the passage. Match the beginning of each sentence to the correct ending. Write the letter in the blank.

A piñata makes a party fun. The idea comes from Mexico. It is part of a game. A piñata can be shaped like an animal. Some look like birds. Some look like dogs. Some look like other animals.

It is easy to make one. First, glue pieces of paper together. Next, color the paper. Then, put treats and toys inside. People take turns trying to break it open. When it breaks, all the treats fall out!

Sentence Beginnings

1. Mexican festivals often have _____.

2. A piñata is made _____.

3. A piñata is often shaped _____.

4. A piñata is filled _____.

Sentence Endings

a. with treats and toys

b. of paper and glue

c. a piñata

d. like an animal

☐ I can ask and answer questions about details in a text.
☐ I can read nonfiction.

Maria's Turn

Read the story. Draw and color pictures that summarize the story.

Maria is excited. The piñata is shaped like a donkey. It hangs from a branch. It is just above her head.

It is Maria's turn. She puts on the blindfold. She swings the stick. She swings again. Crack! The piñata breaks. Treats and toys fall to the ground. Maria and the other children quickly pick them all up.

☐   **I can retell stories with understanding.**

Life in a Tide Pool

Read the story. Circle the correct words to complete the first two sentences. Choose words from the word bank to complete the last sentence.

Word Bank

fish	squid	starfish
sharks	crabs	jellyfish

Samantha stared into a tide pool. Tiny fish swam around the rocks. Two starfish were on the rocks. Four small crabs crawled in the sand. The tide came in and covered the rocky pool. Samantha moved back to the sandy beach.

1. This story is about a girl named _____ .

    Shannon   Samantha   Sasha

2. She was looking at a _____ .

    beach   lake   tide pool

3. She saw _____ , _____ ,

    and _____ .

❑   **I can ask and answer questions about a text I have read.**

Name_____

Look Up!

Read the passage. Circle the correct words to complete the first three sentences. Use the circled words to complete the summary.

It is a helicopter! It flies up. It flies down. It flies forward. It flies backward. It even flies sideways.

A helicopter is useful. It can help rescue people. It can help report traffic and news. It can also lift very big things and move them.

1. This paragraph is about a _____.

    hummingbird   helicopter   airplane

2. It can fly in _____.

    many directions   one direction   two directions

3. It is _____.

    useless   useful

4. This is a text about a _____ . It can fly in

    _____ _____ , so it is

    _____ .

The Right Name

Read the passage. Use the underlined words to complete the summary.

Sometimes, a <u>lizard</u> has a <u>name</u> because of the way he <u>looks</u>. There is an animal called a <u>frilled lizard</u>. He spreads the skin around his neck. It looks like a <u>frilly fan</u>. That is how he got his name. Blue, red, and yellow spots make him colorful.

A _____ can be named for the way he

_____ . The _____

_____ got his _____

because the skin on his neck can spread out to look like a very

_____ _____ .

❑ I can pick out the topic and supporting details.
❑ I can ask and answer questions to figure out the meaning of words and phrases.

What's a Moropus?

Read the passage. Draw a picture in the box of a moropus.

People look at bones to learn about animals from long ago. A moropus is one of those animals. She was a lot like a horse. She was as big as a horse. She also looked like a horse. But, she was different in one big way. She did not have hooves like a horse. Instead, she had claws. She probably used her claws to dig for food. Her front legs were also a little longer than her back legs.

☐   **I can use pictures and words to tell what a text is about.**
☐   **I can read informational texts.**

Paige's Toy Bank

Read the story. Circle the correct word to answer each question.

Paige had been saving money for a long time. She wanted to buy a new kite. She hoped to fly it in the contest on Saturday. The one she wanted was yellow, blue, green, and red. It costs five dollars. Paige opened her toy bank. She poured her money out on the desk. She hoped that she had saved enough.

1. Who is this story about?

    Penny   Paige   Paul

2. What has she been doing?

    flying kites   playing with toys   saving money

3. Why was she saving money?

    for a new toy   to buy a bike   to buy a kite

4. How much does it cost?

    five dollars   two dollars   four dollars

5. Did she have enough money?

    yes   no

☐   I can ask and answer questions about a text I have read.

Platypus

Read the passage. Circle the correct word to answer each question.

There is an animal called a platypus. He lives in Australia. His nickname is Duckbill. That is because he has a mouth that looks like a duck's bill. He also has webbed feet. His flat tail helps him swim. That is kind of like a duck too!

A platypus rests during the day. He wakes up in the evening to hunt for food. He eats worms and other small water animals.

1. Where does the platypus live?

    Australia   Austria   Denver

2. What is the platypus's nickname?

    Donald   Duckbill   Dudley

3. What helps the platypus swim?

    webbed feet   snout   soft fur

4. When does a platypus look for food?

    evening   mid-morning   afternoon

❑ **I can ask and answer questions about details in a text.**
❑ **I can read informational text.**

"Bee" Strong

Read the story. Circle the correct word to answer each question. Use the circled words to complete the summary.

Bobbi Bee landed near a flower. He thought it was pretty and wanted to take the flower home. But, it was much bigger than he was.

Bobbi thought he was very strong. He had to try to lift the flower! He floated over it and grabbed it with all six legs. Bobbi flapped his wings. Up he flew! He was strong!

1. Who is this story about?

   Britney Bee   Bill Bobcat   Bobbi Bee

2. What did he think he was?

   strong   weak   tired

3. What was he trying to lift?

   crumb   flower   cookie

4. How big was it compared to him?

   smaller   bigger   same

5. This is about _____ _____.

   He was _____ enough to lift a _____.

   It was _____ than he was.

☐ **I can ask and answer questions about a text I have read.**
☐ **I can retell stories with understanding.**

Oops!

Read the story. Use the underlined words to complete the summary.

A little gray <u>mouse</u> scampered up to the glass door of a house. His tiny black eyes peeked through the <u>glass</u> <u>door</u>. His pink nose twitched. Inside the house, a <u>cat</u> raised her head and <u>looked</u> out the glass door. This <u>scared</u> the mouse! He turned and <u>raced</u> back to a <u>woodpile</u> nearby. The cat yawned and went back to sleep.

A _____ peeked through a _____ _____ .

A _____ woke up and _____ at the mouse.

The mouse was _____ , so he _____

to a _____ .

❑   **I can retell stories with understanding.**

An Old-Time Train Ride

Read this schedule. Use the schedule to complete the activity on page 41.

Old-Time
Train Ride

Adults $15.00

Children $8.00

Leave **Virginia City**	12:00 pm
Arrive **Gold Hill**	1:00 pm
Arrive **Genoa**	2:00 pm
Arrive **Dayton**	3:00 pm
Arrive **Sutton Creek**	4:00 pm
Return to **Virginia City**	5:00 pm

❏   I can read informational texts.

An Old-Time Train Ride (cont.)

Answer questions about the train schedule. Use your answers to write a summary.

1. Where does the train ride start?_____

2. What time does the train ride begin? _____

3. How many places does the train stop between leaving and returning to Virginia

    City? _____

4. What is the total time of the train ride?_____

5. Write a short summary about the train and its schedule.

    _____

    _____

    _____

❏   I can ask and answer questions about details in a text.
❏   I can use text features to find information.

Pete's Plant

Read the story. Find and circle the underlined words in the puzzle. Use some of the circled words to complete a summary.

Pete planted one tiny seed. Every day he watered the seed. One morning he saw a speck of green. It was a plant! It grew to be three feet tall. A big bud was at the very top. One morning Pete filled the watering can and walked outside. Pete was so happy! The tiny seed was now a big, yellow sunflower!

s	w	a	t	e	r	e	d	n	p	r	t	d	t
e	v	p	g	s	g	m	e	k	g	h	c	r	f
e	v	e	r	i	e	v	e	r	y	l	d	a	y
d	s	t	e	u	r	i	g	a	o	n	j	g	i
o	n	e	w	a	s	u	n	f	l	o	w	e	r
p	l	a	n	t	e	d	b	e	p	l	e	n	i

_____ planted a _____.

He _____ it every _____.

It grew into a big, yellow _____.

☐ I can retell stories with understanding.

What Is the Difference?

Read the sentences. If the sentence tells how the sun and the moon are the same, write **S** on the line. If the sentence tells how the sun and the moon are different, write **D** on the line.

1. _____ The sun is shaped like a ball, and so is the moon.

2. _____ The sun is made of gas, and the moon is made of rock.

3. _____ The sun is a star, but the moon is not.

4. _____ The sun and the moon seem to move across the sky.

5. _____ The moon goes around Earth, but the sun does not.

6. _____ The sun and the moon are far away.

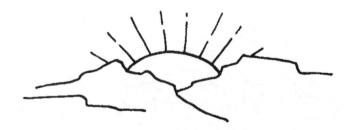

❑ I can tell the things that are the same and different between two texts on the same topic.

Cars and Trucks

Read about cars and trucks. Underline words in each paragraph that tell facts about cars or trucks. Use those words to complete the chart on page 45.

Cars can be fun to drive and have four wheels. Cars use fuel, like gasoline. Cars have trunks to carry things like backpacks and boxes. Cars are made to carry people. Sometimes cars are used by families to go on long trips together. Some cars are used to go really fast. These race cars have room for only one person.

Some people like to drive trucks just because they are big and powerful. Big trucks have 18 wheels. Trucks are often used for work. They carry heavy loads rather than people. They carry heavy loads of cement, wood, and even water. Trucks use lots of fuel to do these jobs.

❑   I can read informational text.

Cars and Trucks (cont.)

Fill in the chart using facts from the last page. Write words telling about cars in the first column. Write words you underlined about trucks in the third column. Write things that are true of both cars and trucks in the middle column.

Cars	Cars and Trucks	Trucks

☐ I can tell how two parts of a text are connected.
☐ I can tell the things that are the same and different between two texts on the same topic.

Time to Explore

Read the paragraphs. Then, circle all the facts about two kinds of explorers.

Long ago, men called explorers sailed across the ocean. They traveled to faraway places. Sometimes they discovered lands like America and Canada. They journeyed to places where sailing ships had never been seen before. They met new people with strange ways. They saw strange birds and plants that did not live in their homelands.

In the 1960s, another kind of explorer, called astronauts, went to the moon. Astronauts needed powerful rockets to get to the moon. Nobody had ever traveled to the moon before. People on Earth watched on television as the first man stepped out on the moon. Walking on the moon was very easy but getting there was very difficult. The astronauts had to bring their own air and water with them because the moon does not have air or water. Living on the moon would be very strange.

Would you like to be an explorer? You might even travel away from Earth and beyond our own solar system! You might choose to stay here to dive down to the bottom of the ocean. You could even discover a place no one else has ever been before!

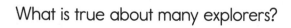

What is true about many explorers?

1. Explorers go places nobody has ever been.

2. Explorers like to stay home.

3. Explorers are curious people, like sailors, pilots, and astronauts, traveling to new places.

4. Explorers often find strange new things when they explore.

5. Explorers go places they have already been.

❑ I can ask and answer questions about details in a text.
❑ I can tell how two parts of a text are connected.
❑ I can read informational texts.

Snick Snacks

Maria and Tyler are comparing their snack recipes. Use the recipes to answer the questions.

Maria's Recipe
1/4 cup chocolate chips
1/4 cup raisins
1/2 cup pecans
2 cups cereal puffs
3/4 cups pretzel pieces
1 cup powdered sugar

Tyler's Recipe
1/4 cup chocolate chips
1/2 cup raisins
1/2 cup peanuts
4 cups cereal puffs
2 cups crushed graham crackers
1 cup powdered sugar

Put chocolate chips in a glass bowl. Place in microwave on high for 1 minute. Take out carefully and stir. Stir raisins and nuts into melted chocolate. Stir in cereal and pretzels or crackers. Place powdered sugar in large storage bag. Add coated cereal. Gently shake until mixture is powdery.

1. Which ingredients are the same in both recipes?

    _____

    _____

    _____

    _____

2. Which ingredients does Tyler need that Maria does not need?

    _____

    _____

3. Which ingredients are the same but are not in the same amounts in the two

    recipes? _____

    _____

❑ **I can tell how two parts of a text are connected.**
❑ **I can tell the things that are the same and different between two texts on the same topic.**

For the Birds

Read the passage. Then, answer the questions.

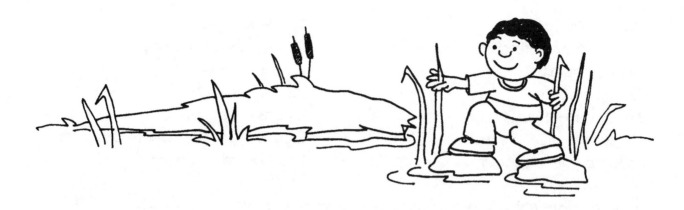

If you wanted a bird for a walking partner, which would you choose: a loon, a swift, or a hummingbird?

None. Loons, swifts, and hummingbirds cannot walk. Swifts can dive faster than most cars ever move. Loons run across the water to start flying. But, a loon can hardly walk on solid ground. Hummingbirds can fly backward, but none of these birds have strong enough legs to support the weight of their bodies. None of these birds would make a good hiking partner.

1. Write a sentence telling how all three of the birds are the same.

    _____

    _____

2. Write a sentence telling how a hummingbird is different from a loon.

    _____

    _____

☐   **I can tell how two parts of a text are connected.**
☐   **I can read informational texts.**

For the Birds Again

Read the paragraphs. Then, answer the question.

A sooty tern can stay in the air for years. After it leaves the nest as a youngster, it stays in the air until it is mature—three to 10 years. Once in a while it may settle on the water for a short period, but it never lands on the ground. When it becomes an adult, it returns to land to begin a family.

Another long flier is the wandering albatross. The albatross has a huge wingspan, as big as 21 feet (6 meters). It can fly tens of thousands of miles to find food for its young. These trips can keep it in the air for months at a time.

1. How are these two birds the same?

    _____

    _____

    _____

☐   I can ask and answer questions about details in a text.
☐   I can tell how two parts of a text are connected.

In and Out

Read the story. Then, answer the questions.

There once lived two monkeys. One was named In. One was named Out. In liked to go out. Out liked to stay in. In was big and black all over. Out was small and had black and white stripes. One day In went out and did not come back in for a long time. Mother Monkey got worried. She told Out to go out and find In.

So Out went out and looked for In. Out found In stuck in a tree. Out went up and helped In down.

When In and Out got home, Mother Monkey asked, "In, where have you been?"

In said, "I was out, stuck up in a tree. But Out came out and helped me get down."

Mother Monkey said, "Good, now Out and In are both in again."

1. Label the animals with the correct names.

_____   _____

2. How are Out and In the same?

_____

_____

3. What was In's problem? _____

_____

☐   I can ask and answer questions about a text I have read.
☐   I can describe characters, settings, and events in a story.
☐   I can compare and contrast characters in stories.

© Carson-Dellosa • CD-104658

Name_____

Great Inventions

Read the two ads. Circle the correct answers to the questions.

The Newest Writing Tool

A personal tool for the 1900s

Handy, little writing tool that is easy to carry

Ready at a moment's notice

Fits in your pocket or purse

Made of lead sandwiched in wood!

Made and sold by 13-year-old Joe Dixon

Best of all, it costs only 5 cents!

The Everything Tool

The latest, from WizKid, Inc.

So much power, all inside a tiny box!

A monitor, keyboard, and color printer

A great help in all your homework

Setup is so easy a kindergartner can do it!

All for the reduced price of $999!

1. Which tool is the smaller tool?

      a. the "newest writing tool" b. the "everything tool"

2. What is the "newest writing tool"?

      a. a computer   b. a pencil

3. What is the "everything tool"?

      a. a computer   b. a pencil

4. Which tools do you have at home and at school?

      a. the newest tool   b. the everything tool   c. both

❑ **I can ask and answer questions about a text I have read.**

Plant Life

Read the two paragraphs. Look at the pictures. Then, answer the questions.

A cactus is from a family of desert plants. They need very little water to grow. These plants have thick main stems, prickly spines, and no leaves. In the spring, they sometimes have flowers. Their roots spread out near the surface to collect rain.

An oak tree is a plant with one big main stem, or trunk, and many branches. Oaks have broad, flat leaves that turn colors in autumn. The seed of an oak tree is the acorn. The roots of an oak grow deep to find groundwater for the tree.

1. Write the name of each plant under its picture. **cactus   oak tree**

2. Which plant would grow in the desert?   **cactus   oak tree**

3. Which plant would grow in a forest?   **cactus   oak tree**

_____   _____

4. How are the cactus and the oak tree alike? Circle the phrases below that describe both the cactus and the oak tree.

    a. has no leaves   b. has prickly spines   c. has a main stem or trunk

    d. needs little water   e. grows branches   f. can have flowers

    g. is a plant   h. has broad, flat leaves   i. grows acorns as seeds

    j. leaves turn colors   k. has underground roots   l. roots collect water

☐   **I can ask and answer questions about details in a text.**
☐   **I can tell the things that are the same and different between two texts on the same topic.**

Not a Match

Read each statement. Circle the word groups that do not fit.

1. Boys and girls can eat all these foods:

   a. apples, oranges, pears

   b. bowl, spoon, soda can

   c. bread, candy, cereal

   d. pudding, carrot, peas

2. These animals do not live in the water:

   a. lion, tiger, bear

   b. fish, sea horse, whale

   c. dog, cat, mouse

   d. elephant, giraffe, bird

3. These are all big:

   a. mouse, dollhouse

   b. ship, plane

   c. planet, sun

   d. mountain, desert

4. These are all small:

   a. baby, puppy

   b. raindrop, snowflake

   c. needle, button

   d. walrus, elephant

5. These words are in ABC order:

   a. fall, grip, happy, into

   b. x-ray, yak, zoo, wagon

   c. push, quack, rush, stay

   d. mister, nice, open, play

☐   **I can tell how parts of a text are connected.**
☐   **I can tell the things that are the same and different between texts on the same topic.**

So They Say

Read each story. Compare the words in **bold print** with the choices below. Circle the choice that means the same as the words in bold print.

Story 1

Jake always did his work late. He wanted to start doing his work on time. Jake wanted to **turn over a new leaf.**

a.   Jake wanted to bring a leaf to school.

b.   Jake wanted to do his work on time.

c.   Jake wanted to turn over his paper.

Story 2

Ana was mad. Her face was red. She would not play with her friends. **She got up on the wrong side of the bed.**

a.   Ana always sleeps on the same side of the bed.

b.   Ana is not used to sleeping in a different bed.

c.   Ana was in a bad mood.

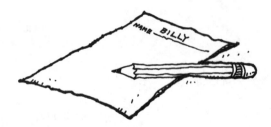

❑   I can point out words and phrases in text that show feeling.

In the Dog House

Read each story. Compare the boldfaced words with the choices below. Circle the choice that means the same as the words in **bold print**.

1. Jake did not close the door when he went out. Flies came into the house. Jake **was in a bad place.**

    a. Jake was in trouble.

    b. Jake went somewhere he should not have gone.

    c. Jake was hot.

2. Michael wanted a garden. He did not know what to plant. He asked José to help him. They looked in books. They went to the store together. They chose great plants. **Two heads are better than one.**

    a. Michael has two heads.

    b. Two boys can find out more than one.

    c. José knows more about plants than Michael.

☐   **I can point out words and phrases in the text that show feeling.**

Wheels, Wheels, Wheels!

Read each story. Circle the letter of the line that completes each sentence. There may be more than one answer to a question.

Wheels help us do work. They make it easy to move things. If cars, trucks, and trains did not have wheels, they could not move. If your scooter did not have wheels, it would not roll.

A long time ago, men and women carried things on their backs. Donkeys and camels carried things in packs. Sometimes, they dragged things along behind them. It was hard to move things without wheels. Men and women could not move very fast or very far. Donkeys and camels could carry only so much weight.

1. Donkeys

   a. use wheels to move.   b. drag loads.

   c. carry packs.   d. can carry heavy loads rapidly.

2. Trucks

   a. use wheels to move.   b. drag loads.

   c. carry packs.   d. can carry heavy loads rapidly.

3. Scooters

   a. use wheels to move.   b. drag loads.

   c. carry packs.   d. can carry heavy loads rapidly.

4. Camels

   a. use wheels to move.   b. drag loads.

   c. carry packs.   d. can carry heavy loads rapidly.

5. It is harder to move things by

   a. using wheels to move.   b. dragging loads.

   c. carrying packs.   d. carrying loads on your back.

☐ **I can tell how two parts of a text are connected.**
☐ **I can read informational texts.**

Tortoise or Turtle?

For this science project, use the underlined facts to complete a poster about tortoises and turtles. Write the facts on page 58.

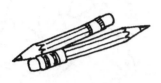 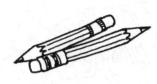

Reptile Fact Sheet

- Tortoises live on land and have front claws for digging.

- Both turtles and tortoises have hard shells.

- Turtles and tortoises both pull their heads into their shells.

- Turtles live in the water and some have semi-webbed feet.

- They both live a long time.

- Turtles and tortoises both lay eggs.

- Some tortoises do not need to drink water.

- There are box turtles and snapping turtles.

❑   I can read informational texts.

Tortoise or Turtle? (cont.)

Fill in the poster using the underlined phrases from the story.

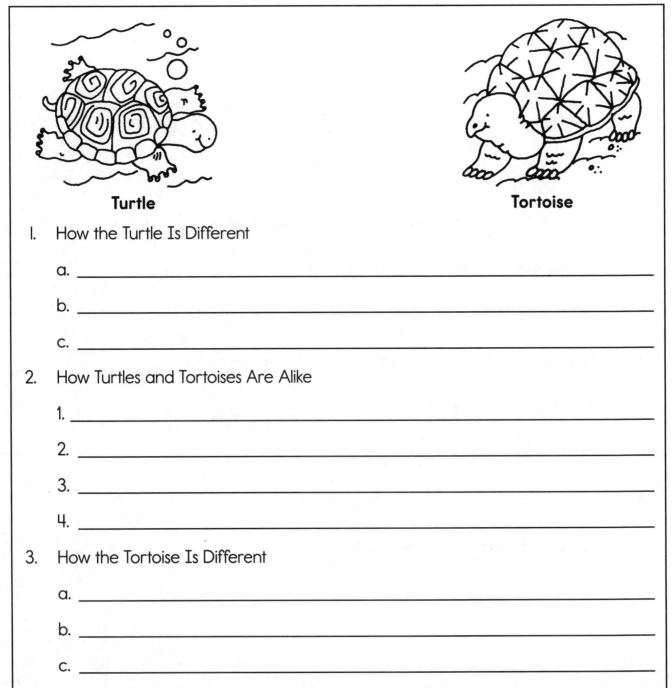

Turtle

Tortoise

1. How the Turtle Is Different

    a. _____

    b. _____

    c. _____

2. How Turtles and Tortoises Are Alike

    1. _____

    2. _____

    3. _____

    4. _____

3. How the Tortoise Is Different

    a. _____

    b. _____

    c. _____

☐   I can tell how two parts of a text are connected.
☐   I can tell the things that are the same and different between two texts on the same topic.

Name_____

Big Mistakes

Read the stories. Answer the cause and effect questions.

William had never climbed a mountain this tall. He thought it would take all morning. It took longer than that. It took all day. What a mistake! He should have packed a lunch. He finally got to the top! He was too hungry to enjoy the view.

1.   William could not enjoy the view from the top of the mountain because _____

_____

_____

Nellie thought she knew enough about the topic to make her speech. She did not make notes. The time for the speech got closer. She still did not make notes. Nellie stood at the front of the class. She could not think of a thing to say! She would never make that mistake again.

2.   Nellie could not give her speech because _____

_____

_____

_____

☐   I can ask and answer questions about a text I have read.
☐   I can read prose and poetry.

Glaciers

Read the article. Match each cause with the correct effect. Write the letter of the effect on the line by the cause.

Glaciers start high in the mountains where lots of snow falls. It stays cold high in the mountains. The snow does not melt. As more snow falls, the flakes pack together. This is like the way snow gets packed together to make a snowball. Snow gets packed so closely that ice forms. When more snow falls, the ice gets thicker and heavier. Then, it begins to slide. The moving ice is called a glacier.

Causes

1. When the ice gets thicker and heavier, _____

2. High in the mountains where it stays cold, _____

3. When the snow packs closely, _____

4. When more snow falls, _____

Effects

a. snow falls.

b. ice forms.

c. the snow packs together.

d. it begins to slide.

☐ I can tell how two parts of a text are connected.
☐ I can read informational texts.

My Emotions

Emotion is another word for feeling. Emotions can be effects. Read the sentences below. Draw a line to match each cause to the correct effect.

Cause

1. When my friend hugged me,

2. When my friend broke my favorite toy,

3. When the lights went out,

4. When I fell down,

5. When all my friends threw me a party,

Effect

a. I felt sad.

b. I felt surprised.

c. I felt loved.

d. I felt afraid.

e. I felt angry.

❑ I can point out words and phrases in the text that show feeling.
❑ I can tell how two parts of a text are connected.

Camping Out

Read the story. Answer the cause and effect questions.

Kayla and Jay were going camping with Dad. They loaded sleeping bags and a camp stove into the van. Mom filled a box with bread, peanut butter, cookies, apples, and chips. Dad carried out the ice chest and a jug of water.

"We are ready to go," he said.

When they got to the state park, Kayla and Jay helped Dad set up camp.

"Bring me the tent," Dad said.

Jay looked in the van. "It's not here."

"Oh, no!" cried Kayla. "We forgot the tent. We will have to go home."

"No," Dad said. "It's a nice, warm night. And it's not going to rain. We will roll our sleeping bags out on the ground. The sky will be our tent."

"Hurray!" shouted Kayla and Jay.

1. Why did Kayla think they would have to go home? _____

   _____

   _____

2. Why did they get to stay? _____

   _____

   _____

3. What did they use as a tent? _____

   _____

   _____

4. What do you think will happen if it rains?_____

   _____

   _____

☐ I can ask and answer questions about a a text that I have read.
☐ I can read prose and poetry.

Letter to Grandma

Read the letter. Circle the correct causes and effects to finish the sentences. There may be more than one answer to a question.

Dear Grandma,

      I did not go to school today because it snowed a lot. I wanted to go outside as soon as I woke up. Mom said it was too cold.

      Later, I put on my jacket, my mittens, my hat, and a scarf.

      I could not go sledding because I broke my sled. I made a snowman instead. Do you like to make snowmen? I drew a picture of the snowman because it will melt soon. His eyes are pinecones. Can you guess what I used for a mouth?

                         Love,

                         Danny

1. It snowed, so Danny

    a. did not have to go to school.

    b. had to stay inside all day.

    c. could not go sledding.

    d. had to wear warm clothes.

    e. decided to make a snowman.

2. Danny put on a jacket, mittens, hat, and scarf

    a. because it was cold outside.

    b. because he was going sledding.

    c. because he was going to play in the snow.

    d. because he wanted to see Grandma.

☐   **I can ask and answer questions about a text I have read.**
☐   **I can point to the text that describe parts of a story.**

A Picnic

Read the story. Circle the correct causes and effects to finish the sentences.

One sunny day, Mrs. Ant said, "Let's go to the park for a picnic."

"Good idea," said Mr. Ant. "Families will be eating there."

"Can we go now?" asked Abe Ant. "I am hungry."

"I don't want to go," said Amy Ant.

"Why not?" asked Mrs. Ant.

"Last time we did not find any food," Amy said.

"This time we might find lots of food," said Abe.

Everyone followed Mrs. Ant to the park. They walked under a picnic table. The four ants sat down. Then, they all looked up. They waited.

1. The Ants went to the park for a picnic because

    a. the park was pretty.

    b. families eat in the park.

2. Abe Ant wanted to go because

    a. he could play in the grass.

    b. he was hungry.

3. Amy Ant did not want to go because

    a. sometimes people do not leave food.

    b. sometimes people step on ants.

4. The Ant family sat under the picnic table and looked up

    a. to watch the sky.

    b. to wait for food to drop down.

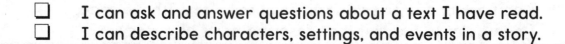

❏ I can ask and answer questions about a text I have read.
❏ I can describe characters, settings, and events in a story.

Lisa's Big Win

Read the story. Write the answers to the cause and effect questions.

Lisa and Jayla were playing in a soccer game. Lisa was good. She could make goals. Her friend Jayla was not playing well. The game was almost over. Their team was losing. Jayla was not helping out.

"You think too much," Lisa told Jayla. "Just kick the ball."

Jayla frowned. Lisa felt bad. She wanted Jayla to be good too. She knew Jayla could play better. Her friend was just nervous.

Lisa got the ball. "Follow me," she told Jayla. Jayla did.

Lisa charged at the goal. The goalie jumped in front of Lisa. Lisa was a star. The goalie knew she would try to score. "Take my pass!" Lisa shouted. She kicked the ball sideways. Jayla caught it with her foot. She shot at the goal.

The ball went in!

Jayla never got another goal, but she played well. She laughed and smiled.

Her team lost, but Lisa still felt like a winner because she helped a friend.

1. Why did Lisa think Jayla was not playing well?

   Lisa thought Jayla was not playing well because _____

   _____

2. What caused Lisa to pass the ball to Jayla?

   Lisa passed the ball to Jayla because _____

   _____

3. What effect did Lisa's pass have on the goalie?

   Because Lisa was a star, the goalie _____

   _____

4. What caused Lisa to feel like a winner even though they lost?

   Lisa felt like a winner because _____

   _____

☐ I can ask and answer questions about a text I have read.
☐ I can point out words and phrases that show feeling.
☐ I can point to the text that describes parts of a story.

Erin's Report Card

Read the story. Look at Erin's report card. Circle the answers to the cause and effect questions.

Erin had ideas about how to do things. When the teacher said what to do, Erin had a better way. Once the teacher said, "Glue the dried beans inside the lines." Erin knew they would be better outside the lines. The lunch monitor said, "Eat slowly." Erin ate quickly. When recess came, her friends wanted to play on the slide. Erin played on the swings instead.

Report Card

Reading	☆	Gets along with others	☆
Writing	☆	Follows directions	☹
Spelling	☆	Listens carefully	☹
Math	☆		Mrs. Murphy

1. What was the cause of Erin's low grades?

    a. She did things her own way.

    b. She talked too much in class.

    c. She did not get along with others.

2. Erin did not follow directions because

    a. she could not listen.

    b. she did not understand.

    c. she thought she had a better way to do things.

3. We know Erin is a good student because

    a. Mrs. Murphy gave her mostly good grades.

    b. she got a sad face in "Follows directions."

☐   I can ask and answer questions about a text I have read.
☐   I can point to the text that describes parts of a story.

School Program

Read the story. Look at the schedule. Circle the answers to the cause and effect questions.

It is the day before the school program. The teachers are ready. They took all the poetry books out of the school library. They put the books in the classrooms. The students will read poems about trees!

The teachers dug holes so that students could plant trees. The first graders made paper leaves for the costumes. They wanted to look like trees in the parade!

It is the day of the program! Here is what happens:

9:00   Students read tree poems.

9:05   Fifth graders planted four trees.

9:30   Fourth graders presented "Why We Love Trees."

9:45   First graders presented "Parade of Leaves."

10:00   Recess spent playing under the trees!

1.   All the poetry books in the school library were checked out because
   a. the students love poetry.
   b. students were reading tree poems.

2.   The teachers dug four deep holes the day before the program so
   a. students could plant four trees.
   b. students could jump in and out of them.

3.   The first graders taped leaves on their shirts for their parade of trees so
   a. they could look funny.
   b. they could look like trees.

☐   **I can ask and answer questions about a text I have read.**
☐   **I can point to the text that describes parts of a story.**

Windy Farm

Read the story. Circle the answers to the cause and effect questions on page 69.

Three friends lived on Windy Farm. There was Harry the Horse, Dustin the Dog, and Olivia the Owl. Each of them wanted to build a new house. A house would keep them safe when the wind blew.

Harry made his house out of straw. He loved to eat straw! A house made of his favorite food would be good. When the wind blew hard, his house fell over! Harry felt sad.

Dustin made his house out of sticks. He loved to fetch sticks! A house made of his favorite toy would be good. When the wind blew even harder, some sticks fell off. Holes were in his walls! Dustin howled.

Olivia was a wise owl. She knew to make a house out of bricks. However, Olivia was not strong enough to carry bricks. Harry and Dustin were, though.

"We can build a house together," Olivia said. "Will you help me?"

Harry and Dustin helped Olivia make a house out of bricks. No matter how hard the wind blew, their house stayed strong!

❑   I can read prose and poetry.

Windy Farm (cont.)

1. Three friends wanted to build houses because

   a. they liked the farm.

   b. they wanted to make new friends.

   c. they wanted to stay safe.

2. Why did Harry make a house out of straw?

   a. Straw was strong.

   b. He liked to eat straw.

   c. He did not know what else to use.

3. Why did Dustin build a house of sticks?

   a. Because the sticks were strong.

   b. Because he did not like straw.

   c. Because he loved to fetch sticks.

4. Why did Olivia need help from her friends?

   a. Because she could not carry bricks on her own.

   b. Because she was afraid.

   c. Because she did not know what to do.

5. Why couldn't the wind knock over Olivia's house?

   a. Because the wind did not blow hard enough.

   b. Because brick is strong.

   c. Because the friends worked together.

☐ **I can ask and answer questions about a text I have read.**
☐ **I can describe the characters, settings, and events in a story.**
☐ **I can point to the text that describes parts of a story.**

Play Ball

Read the story. Write the answers to the cause and effect questions.

Camden had an idea. His school did not have a soccer team. He and his friends could make their own league. The neighborhood had enough kids for four teams. His friends agreed. "What a great idea!" they said.

It took all day to clear a vacant lot. Camden wanted the field to be smooth. "Nobody will want to play on a bad field," Camden said. "We have to make it fair." He made sure the goal posts were the same on each side. He counted his steps to measure the field. He made sure the ball had lots of air.

When the day came for the first game, everybody came. They all wanted to play, even Camden. But, he did not.

"Why won't you play?" a friend asked.

"Because we need rules," Camden said. "So today, I'll be the ref."

His friend, Ben, smiled. "I'll do it next time," he said.

Camden smiled back.

1. Why did Camden and his friends make their own league?

_____

_____

2. What did Camden think would be the effect of a bad field?

_____

_____

3. What caused Camden to choose not to play?

_____

_____

4. When Camden's friend said he would be ref next time, what was the effect?

_____

_____

☐ **I can ask and answer questions about a text I have read.**
☐ **I can read prose and poetry.**

Perry's Treasure Hunt

Read the story. Circle the clue words (**because**, **so**, **why**, and **when**) in the story. Answer the cause and effect questions on page 72.

One spring day, Perry Packrat said, "I think I will go looking for things. I need more stuff to put in my room."

Perry walked down the forest trail. She took her wagon so she could put all the things she found in it.

Perry looked to the left. She looked to the right. She looked up above her. She looked down at her feet. She saw a stack of bottle caps. She scooped them up and put them in her wagon.

"No, no! Don't take my bottle caps!" yelled Shelby Squirrel. "I am going to paste them on a picture for my teacher. That is why I have been saving them."

Perry walked down the path with her wagon. She saw a stack of newspapers in front of Rick Raccoon's den. So, she asked, "Do you need all these papers, Mr. Raccoon?"

"I am saving them so I can start warm fires this winter. I need them," he said.

Perry was sad because she wanted the papers too. She walked on. When she saw some pretty flowers, she wanted to pick them for her mother. Her mother loved flowers.

Perry started to pick a flower. A bee buzzed by. "Please do not pick the flowers. I need the flowers so I can make honey."

Perry went home with her empty wagon.

Mama opened the front door. "Where have you been?" she asked.

She saw Perry's empty wagon. Mama smiled because she was happy. Perry had not come home with more trash!

❏ **I can read prose and poetry.**

Perry's Treasure Hunt (cont.)

Answer the questions about the story on page 71.

1. Why did Perry take her wagon? _____

    _____

2. Why had Shelby saved the bottle caps?_____

    _____

3. Why did Rick Raccoon need the papers? _____

    _____

4. Why did the bee need the flowers?_____

    _____

5. What made Mama smile? _____

    _____

❑ I can ask and answer questions about a text I have read.
❑ I can describe the characters, settings, and events in a story.
❑ I can point to the text that describes parts of a story.

Write On!

Read the sentence pairs below. Combine the two sentences into one sentence that tells cause and effect. Use a cause and effect clue word. **Because, so, why,** and **when** are clue words.

1. Tony spilled his milk.

    Mom got mad.

    _____

    _____

2. The big dog barked at Tia.

    She ran home crying.

    _____

    _____

3. The little bird could not get back to its nest.

    It could not fly.

    _____

    _____

4. Joanne kicked the ball into the street.

    She ran to tell the teacher.

    _____

    _____

❏   **I can retell phrases with understanding.**

Chain Reaction

Read the story. Answer the questions about cause and effect.

Tracy dropped the marble. It hit the sleeping cat on the nose. The surprised cat jumped on the dog's tail. The dog yipped and chased the cat. The cat ran under the fish tank. The fish tank shook back and forth. Water and one small fish splashed out onto the floor. The thirsty dog lapped up the water.

1. Why did the dog lap up the water?_____

    _____

2. Why did the fish tank wobble?_____

    _____

3. Why did the dog chase the cat? _____

    _____

4. Why did the cat jump on the dog's tail?_____

    _____

5. What caused the chain reaction?_____

    _____

❑   **I can ask and answer questions about a text I have read.**

As Days Grow Short

Read the story. Think about clues in the sentences. Use the clues to infer the answers to the questions.

Judd saw an animal with a gray tail climb down from a tree branch. It raced across the ground and picked up an acorn. It ran back to the tree and hid the acorn in a hole in the tree trunk. Judd knew the animal was storing food to eat during the winter.

The animal came back out from the tree trunk and ran away. Judd chased it to see where it would go. His feet made crunching sounds in the leaves on the ground.

Circle the correct answers below.

1. The gray animal is a

    squirrel.   brown bear.   rabbit.

    How do you know?_____

2. Storing food means

    eating lots of food.   saving food.   giving food away.

    How do you know?_____

3. What season is it?

    winter   autumn   spring

    How do you know?_____

☐   **I can describe characters, settings, and events in a story.**
☐   **I can point to the text that describes parts of a story.**

Take-Along Home

Read the story. Use clues in the story to infer the answers to the questions.

Taron was ready to go for his morning walk. He peeked outside and looked around the yard.

"Where is Sam?" Taron asked. He wanted to take a nice, quiet walk by himself. He did not want that pesky Sam following him. He could not see Sam anywhere.

Taron walked slowly across the grass. He looked for bright red flowers. They were his favorite food.

Someone made a noise nearby. "Sniff, sniff." The sound got louder and louder.

Oh, no! Taron thought. *It is Sam. He is coming this way.* Taron stood very still.

Sam found him anyway. Sam sniffed Taron's feet. Sam licked Taron's nose. Taron did not like that. Taron pulled his feet and head into his shell. Sam barked at him. Taron was happy that he was safe inside his take-along home.

Draw a picture of Taron	Draw a picture of Sam

1. Circle the clues that tell you what animal Taron is.

   Taron pulled his head   Taron listened.   Taron looked for bright
   and feet into his shell.   red flowers.

2. Circle the clues that tell you what animal Sam is.

   Sam sniffed.   Sam barked.   Sam found Taron.

☐ **I can describe characters, settings, and events in a story.**
☐ **I can point to the text that describes parts of a story.**
☐ **I can read prose and poetry.**

A Trip to the Farm

Read each story. Read the three endings. Use clues in the story to infer which ending makes sense. Circle the correct answers.

1. Jan's class was going on a trip. They were going to the farm. A big bus came to get them.

    a. They all went home

    b. They got on the bus.

    c. They went out to play.

2. They rode for a long time. The bus came to a stop. They were at the farm!

    a. They all got off.

    b. They went to the store.

    c. They got on top of the bus.

3. They explored the farm. They went to see the horse. He had a long mane. Jan gave him a carrot.

    a. He ate the carrot.

    b. He neighed.

    c. He galloped away.

❑   I can retell stories with understanding.

Playground Fun

Read the list of playground activities. Read each story. Choose the activity that best fits each story. Write the name of the game on the blank line.

the swing set	the slide	the sandbox
the seesaw	hide-and-go-seek	

1. Erica climbed the ladder. She stood on the top step and looked down at the playground. Erica sat and gave herself a push. Erica was playing on _____

   _____

2. Andrew took toys out of his backpack. He handed a dump truck to his little brother. Andrew chose a shovel. He wanted to build a road and a castle. Andrew and his brother were playing in _____

3. Mia and Lucy wanted to play. They both sat. "Hold on tight," Mia said. Mia pushed her feet against the ground. Lucy laughed as she sank. Mia lifted toward the sky. Mia and Lucy were playing on _____

   _____

4. Connor closed his eyes. He began to count to 20. He heard the footsteps of his friends as they scattered. Connor knew he would find them. "Ready or not, here I come," shouted Connor. Connor was playing _____

   _____

5. Melanie loves to go high. She pulled on the chains and kicked out with her legs. She felt like she was flying. Melanie was playing on _____

   _____

☐	I can describe characters, settings, and events in a story.
☐	I can read prose and poetry.

Pets on Parade

Read the riddles. Can you guess what pet each child has? Choose a word from the word bank to complete each sentence.

Word Bank				
bird	fish	lizard	snake	spider

Jenna said, "My pet is named Polly. She has green, orange, and yellow feathers. She has a sharp beak and she can fly."

"My pet is named Goldie," Bailey said. "She has big eyes and fins. She lives in a tank. I cannot hold her, but I love to look at her."

Maggie said, "My pet has eight legs. I call him Fuzzy because he has a furry body and furry legs. Some people think my pet can poison you with a bite, but he cannot!"

"My pet is Lizzy," Robert said. "She loves to eat insects. She's a reptile. If you pull on her tail, it might fall off. Do not worry! If it does, she will grow a new one."

Nell said, "I have a pet named Slider. Slider has no legs, just a long, skinny body. His tongue flicks in and out. He swallows his food whole."

1. Polly is a _____

2. Goldie is a _____

3. Fuzzy is a _____

4. Lizzy is a _____

5. Slider is a _____

☐ **I can describe characters, settings, and events in a story.**
☐ **I can read prose and poetry.**

Cookie Jar

Read the story. Use the clues in the story to answer the questions. Circle or write the correct answers.

"Holly, why did you eat so many cookies?" Heather asked.

"I did not eat any cookies," Holly said. "You must have eaten them all!"

"I did not," Heather said.

Each girl was sure the other had eaten most of the cookies. They were angry at each other. They stopped talking and playing together.

Later, when Heather walked across the dining room, she almost stepped on a cookie. "What is this doing here?" she asked. She walked down the hall and knocked on Holly's door.

"Holly! Look what I found on the floor."

"On the floor? How did it get there?" Holly asked.

"I don't know," Heather said, "but we will find out."

The girls got four more cookies from the jar and set them out on a plate. They hid in the closet.

Edgar trotted in. He jumped up on a chair, put both front paws on the table, and picked up a cookie. He jumped down and padded out the door with his treat.

Heather and Holly laughed and said, "Now we know who took the cookies."

1. Who are Holly and Heather?

    friends   brothers   sisters

    What clues told you who they are? _____

    _____

2. How do they feel at the beginning of the story?_____

3. How do they feel at the end of the story?_____

4. Who is Edgar?

    a little brother   a dog   a bird

5. What clues told you who Edgar is?_____

    _____

❏   I can ask and answer questions about a text I have read.
❏   I can point out words and phrases in the text that show feeling.

Bug Catcher

Read the story. Circle, write, or draw the answers to the questions.

Lizzie and I decided to hunt bugs. I got a jar and I punched some holes in the lid. Lizzie and I went out to the backyard.

"Where should we look?" I asked. Lizzie's tongue flicked out. It looked like she was pointing to bushes near the porch. Lizzie perched on my shoulder. We got down and crawled under the bushes.

It was dark and damp. We sat very quietly, watching for bugs. I found two ants. I dropped them into the jar.

"You guard the jar, Lizzie. I'll get more bugs." I found a caterpillar and put it in the jar. Then, I saw a small, gray spider. It scurried away. I crawled after it, but the spider got away.

I checked the other bugs we'd caught, but they had all disappeared!

Complete the following.

1. Lizzie is a

    cat. bird. lizard.

2. Draw a picture of Lizzie.

3. How do you think the children felt when all the bugs disappeared? Why?

    _____

    _____

    _____

❑ **I can describe characters, settings, and events in a story.**
❑ **I can point out words and phrases in the text that show feeling.**

Alisha Jones, Private Eye

Read the story below. Use clues in the story to infer the answers to the questions on page 83.

Alisha hung a sign outside her clubhouse door. It said:

Alisha Jones, Private Eye

Noah, her neighbor, rode down the driveway. He was on his tricycle. He looked at the sign for a long time. He looked around the yard.

"Where is the yard sale?" he asked.

"There is no yard sale," Alisha said.

"But you have a sign up," Noah said.

Alisha said, "That sign says I am a detective. I solve crimes and I find things that are lost."

"If I lost something, could you find it?" Noah asked.

"I could try," Alisha said.

Noah took Alisha to his house. They went to his room.

Alisha looked around. Toys were everywhere! She was not surprised Noah had lost something. She was surprised he ever found anything.

Noah went over to his closet. He took out a plastic car. It had a slot in the top.

"This is my bank," he said. "Every week I get ten dimes for my allowance. I spend five of them at the mall. I put the other five in here. On Monday, I had a lot of dimes. Now they are all gone! Can you find them for me?"

"First, we need some clues," Alisha said. She shook the bank. She did not hear any dimes. She opened the little door on the bottom of the bank. Two pieces of paper fell out. One was white and one was green. When she read what was written on the white paper, she tried not to laugh. It said:

Dear Noah,

I needed some change for the wash. You had $4.70 in dimes. Here is $5.00.

Thank you.

Love,

Mom

☐   **I can read prose and poetry.**

Be a Private Eye

1. How old do you think Noah is?_____

    How can you tell? _____

    _____

2. Why do most people put up homemade signs on Alisha's street?

    _____

    How can you tell?

    _____

3. Was Noah's room messy or neat?

    _____

    How can you tell?

    _____

4. What was the green piece of paper in Noah's bank?

    _____

❑   **I can describe characters, settings, and events in a story.**

So They Say

Read each story. Circle the choice that means the same as the words in **bold print.**

1. Juan had lots of homework. He also had a new CD. He decided to listen to it while he did his homework. That way, he could **kill two birds with one stone.**

    a. Juan wanted to throw stones at birds.

    b. Juan was going to skip his homework.

    c. Juan wanted to listen to his CD and get his homework done at the same time.

2. Alexa was tired. She had gotten up at dawn. She had cheerleading after school. Then, she did her homework. She decided it was time to **hit the sack.**

    a. Alexa was ready to get up and face the day.

    b. Alexa is ready to go to bed.

    c. Alexa wanted to punch something.

☐   I can ask and answer questions to figure out the meaning of words and phrases.